CULTIVATE
COURAGE

FACE FEAR. FULFILL DREAMS.

Praise for *Cultivate Courage*

Dave asked me to write a blurb for his book. My first thought was, "Why would anyone care what I think about his book?" Then a voice in my brain said, "Yeah, but you're a comic, so you should be able to write something clever. You know … the kind of thing that Steve Martin writes on the back of books." I liked that idea until the voice continued, "Of course you're no Steve Martin. Just tell Dave you don't have time. He'll understand." Then I started reading the manuscript. Now that voice in my brain is whimpering as I write simply … There's a real good chance this book will change your life!

—BOB STROMBERG, COMIC/WRITER

Have you ever had that gnawing feeling of not being good enough—consumed with an irrational fear? You are not alone. Dave Cornell in *Cultivate Courage* hits this topic head on with his personal stories, humor, and Christian faith. He offers practical suggestions on how to remove the boulders in your life and start living courageously.

—JAN HAEG, DIRECTOR, LIFETOUCH MEMORY MISSION

Courage. It's the one choice that will make a difference. We think courage, though, is something we should feel. And that strength must accompany our willingness to be courageous. Dave Cornell, however, unveils the truth. Fear isn't what holds us back. It's what we say to ourselves in the midst of fear that stops us. And in this groundbreaking book, Dave shares a powerful framework to help you face those fears and challenges, and discover the treasure that's waiting for you! You have a choice: Live courageously, or live in fear. This book helps you live courageously!

—PAUL GUSTAVSON, AUTHOR, *LEADERS PRESS ON*

Through stories and practical steps, Dave will take you on a personal journey from fear into courage. Dave will give you a call-to-action and a plan so you can step past your own fears to begin your journey of living the courageous life.

—MICHAEL WOODWARD, JUMBLETHINK

When I first heard Dave speak, I did not expect him to drag me to the edge of my chair … jaw on the ground, heart in my hands. But he did. He's about to do the same for you. The best part of it all? By the end of Dave's book, your jaw will be back in its place, your heart will tucked safely back where it belongs, and you will be standing tall … braver, stronger, and ready to chase your dreams courageously.

—CATHERINE BYERS BREET, CHIEF STRIPE CHANGER, ARBEZ

CULTIVATE
COURAGE
FACE FEAR. FULFILL DREAMS.

DAVE CORNELL

Cultivate Courage
Copyright 2018 by Dave Cornell

Printed in the United States of America.
First edition; second printing.
ISBN 978-1-7321973-2-9—Print
ISBN 978-1-7321973-3-6—eBook
ISBN 978-1-7321973-4-3—Audio book

Cover design: Amy Cornell
Cover photo: Sasin Tipchai
Quotes design: Kaitlyn Cornell
Book design: Sue Filbin

Thank you for permission to use quoted material from these authors:
Dr. Brené Brown, www.brenebrown.com
Jack Canfield, www.jackcanfield.com
Donald Miller, www.storybrand.com

Visit:
www.cultivatecourage.com
www.minnesotaspeakers.com/speaker.php?sid=171

Disclaimer:
The material presented here is of a general nature. Readers should not act on the basis of any information without considering professional advice with due regard to their own particular circumstances.

Dedication

This book is dedicated to my wife, Amy.
She has had the courage to stick with me for better,
for worse, for richer, for poorer, in sickness and in health.
Thank you, Amy Lou! ILYMTYWEK!

Foreword

When I was twelve years old, I loved riding my horse Cojo. That horse loved to run and I loved to ride fast. I remember galloping in the field while my dad drove the pick-up truck on the dirt road alongside of me, seeing how fast I could go. With windows down, he shouted, "Twenty miles per hour, twenty-five … thirty." Adrenaline rush!

On a certain day, I was riding Cojo by myself across a field of lush, green alfalfa hay. There was a problem. The hay was about two feet tall but the irrigation pipe was about 18 inches tall, meaning the horse could not see the irrigation pipe from a distance. We were at a flat run when Cojo noticed the irrigation pipe, stopped on a dime, and reared out of fear. My momentum carried me. I flew off the horse, except for one thing: My left foot went forward in the saddle stirrup and got stuck. I was on the ground but my left foot was stuck in the stirrup.

The awkward tugging of the saddle can make even a good horse mad. Cojo took off bucking and running, dragging me under him. I was sure to get stepped on or dragged over a rock—in fact, my father had warned me to keep my toes up and heels down in the saddle because he had seen a neighbor get dragged home, dead, exactly this way. I was being dragged through the field under a big horse. My trying to pull myself up and out of the saddle just made Cojo more crazy. And then, in an instant, I fell out of the stirrup onto the bed of fresh green alfalfa. I was spared. I could hardly breathe. I felt my limbs. Nothing was broken. I was free. I was safe. I had made it.

From a quarter-mile away, my dad and a friend had seen what had happened. They caught and led Cojo to me. Once they noticed that I was okay, Dad said, "You better get back on the horse." I immediately replied, "Are you kidding me? I just almost died."

He wasn't kidding. We both knew that you can ruin a horse if you get thrown off and don't get back on, as the horse might always think they can buck you off with no consequence. I was scared. I did not feel like getting back on. In spite of how I felt and the healthy fear of horses that came after that accident, I got back on and rode Cojo home.

My dad gave me the gift of his encouragement that day. He compassionately, but clearly, pushed me to have courage. That gift started my courage muscle that would give me strength to move forward in times when I was called names, treated unfairly, and lost a business. I wish I could say I always made the courageous choice. I wish I had always stood up for those who could not stand up for themselves, or had taken the risk that was the harder-but-better choice.

I can say I would not be where I am today without courage. One can have fear without courage, but one cannot have courage without fear. Courage is about stepping forward into your fear—and even in spite of it. It turns out, I have had to get up on that figurative horse over and over, even when I've been full of fear.

After my wife and I lost all of our money on a business, after repeatedly being turned down by publishers and agents for my first book, after accepting my first consulting contracts with Fortune 500 global leadership teams, I see the need for courage in the face of fear. I face fear every day. And I ask myself, "Can I deliver on my promises, can I make the impact I hope to make, can I build the company I hope to build, am I doing all I can to raise my kids and be the best father, husband, and friend?"

People who know me and my work at Trust Edge Leadership Institute know that all of my work centers around an 8-Pillar framework for building trusted leaders and organizations. The 8 Pillars came out of my graduate studies and our ongoing research to help organizations be the most trusted in their industry. The 8 Pillars all start with the letter C, so some people ask me, "If there was a ninth pillar, what would it be?" Without hesitation I say, "Courage."

To build any of the pillars actually first takes courage. To do what is right over what is easy, to show compassion when you really don't like or agree with the other person, and to take a smart risk or do anything of lasting value—all start by having courage!

I know Dave Cornell and his work on courage. I not only

count him a dear friend, but I have hired him, so I clearly believe in his character and work. Dave is authentic and real—the same on stage and off. What I love about his work on courage is that he gives real, actionable tools for framing fear and living more courageously.

The first thing we all need to have, if we are ever going to get from where we are to where we want to be, is courage. It's time to get back on the horse.

—DAVID HORSAGER, CEO, TRUST EDGE LEADERSHIP INSTITUTE

Table of Contents

The Value of a Crisis

Name Your Fear

Frame Your Fear

Claim Your Courage

Courage is a heart issue.

DAVE CORNELL

Introduction

Fear is something we all face but we rarely, if ever, talk seriously about with anyone else. We all want to be people who at least appear to have it all together, yet it surprises me how often in regular conversation people will say something like, "Oh, I could never do that. I'd be too afraid."

Now it's important to point out early that I'm not talking about fear of snakes or fear of heights or fear of spiders. I'm not talking about climbing Mt. Kilimanjaro or running a marathon or building your own house. Instead, I'm referring to fears about living out our dreams and becoming who we were created to be.

This is a book about irrational fear—a fear that keeps us from stepping out of our comfort zone by doing something courageous. Courage is a word that seems to be most often reserved for heroic actions such as those performed by police officers, fire fighters, and soldiers. Courageous acts are acts that put people on the nightly news and in newspaper headlines. Their stories go viral on the Internet.

The courageous act may have been pulling someone from a flaming car or a burning building. Perhaps someone rescued a small child from an attack by a vicious dog while putting his own life in danger. Those are all truly courageous acts and deserve all the glory and publicity they get.

But this isn't a book about facing those types of fears; instead, this is a book is about performing courageous acts in your everyday life, whether in your personal life or your professional life. This book is about facing those nagging voices in your head when you lie down to go to sleep at night.

This book is about facing the demons of needing to meet others' expectations, of self-defeating attitudes, and of feeling unworthy. It's about the need to please others and get out of your own way. It's about facing the voices that chide you for not being the lone voice of dissent during that meeting, or for letting your kids off the hook (again) and not holding them accountable as you said you would, or for not at least applying for the job that could be just what you've been seeking for years. It's about learning to believe in yourself, a little bit at a time.

A major premise of this book is this: One can have fear without courage, but one cannot have courage without fear. You see, I believe one of the reasons we don't talk about our irrational fears is because, on some level, we realize them to be irrational. Let me give you an example:

Jane, not her real name, waited patiently as others visited with me after I had given a presentation on courage to a group of nursing students. Jane is the lady who actually had invited me to come and address the group. I thought she was waiting to thank me for being there and make sure I had everything I needed before heading home.

She did thank me, but then she started to tell me about how my presentation had impacted her. "I have a nine-year-old granddaughter. On the first Saturday of every month, we go to the Mall of America to spend time together. We get there about 9:45, just before it opens," she said. Jane continued, "The first place we go is Cinnabon. We get our roll and sit down and go through our day—where we're going to shop, where we're going to have lunch, what ride she's going on, and any other details.

"We finish up our rolls and, by now, the stores are open so we begin our day. Often, when we come out of a store, my granddaughter will see an escalator. She loves to ride escalators. She'll say, "Grandma, Grandma, there's an escalator. Let's go ride the escalator!"

Jane shared her fear of escalators. "Dave, I'm scared to death of escalators. When we come out and she sees one, I do whatever I can to divert her attention. I'll point her in the direction of another store that's on our list or I'll tell her I just need to sit down for a few minutes. I do everything I can to distract her from the escalator. I know where every elevator and every stairwell is in the Mall. Hearing you today made me realize that I am denying my granddaughter something that she loves."

Jane went on to tell me that the next Saturday, she and her granddaughter didn't plan to be together. She said she was going to go the Mall and learn to ride the escalator so she could do it with her granddaughter the next time they went together!"

Most of us might think to ourselves, "How can she be afraid of riding an escalator? That's just stupid!" But to her, the fear is very real. And while she knows how irrational it is, to share it would only add to her shame and/or embarrassment about this fear. Ultimately, you will see that what was necessary to overcome her fear is the same process that will help you overcome yours.

The fact is, fear and courage are very personal journeys. If you Google the terms "living fearlessly" or "fearless living," you will get over half a million sites to choose from on how to lead a fearless life. However, this book isn't about living fearlessly. In fact, I believe that if you wait to become fearless before moving forward, you'll never move forward at all!

It's important to recognize that fear will always be present in some form. Courage is about stepping into your fear in spite of it. It's about taking control of the fear and not letting the fear control you. Courage is similar to a muscle. You'll begin to find that, as you take courageous steps, it becomes easier to act courageously. I won't say it will become easy, just that it will become easier as you begin to step out and find that the things you feared aren't as scary as you first thought.

One of my favorite quotes about courage comes from John Wayne, the grizzled movie cowboy from my youth. Wayne said, "Courage is being scared to death but saddling up anyway!" So if you aren't living your dreams or are stuck in a rut and often saying, "Someday I'm going to … " then this book is for you.

Introduction

While this book is written in a secular fashion, at its core is Biblical truth. Joshua 1:9 has been the inspiration for this entire project as I saw this verse play itself out in my life. "Have I not commanded you? Be strong and courageous! Do not be afraid; do not be discouraged. For the Lord your God will be with you wherever you go."

I wish you well on your journey to a more courageous life!

We can have fear without courage,
but we cannot have courage without fear.

DAVE CORNELL

Chapter 1

Cowardly or Courageous?

It was the summer of 1961. I was six years old, watching my eight-year-old brother Phil's baseball game on the field behind West Ward Elementary School in Wahoo, Nebraska. Phil's team had just finished batting in the top half of the last inning. They were taking the field, and if they could get the other team out without their scoring any runs, his team would win the game.

Quickly, they got the first two outs. I was standing directly behind the batter, catcher, and umpire behind home plate. The backstop was made of chain-link fence. It was the kind of fence that, as a fan with no seat, you would put your fingers through and hold onto as you watched the game.

Occasionally, the umpire would turn around and tell us to keep our fingers out of the fence. He was concerned there might be a foul tip or a wild throw that might catch our fingers and pinch them to the fence. It was one of those things that I'd never heard of happening but if it did, yikes, it would hurt and probably break a finger—or worse!

I was with my two best friends, Dennis and Doug. As the next batter was coming to the plate, we all recognized this player was one of the better players on the other team and could easily hit a home run and tie the game. We also knew that Billy, last name unknown, was considered a tough guy, a bully. He was the same age as my brother but went to East Ward Elementary, on the other side of town, so we didn't know much more about him than his reputation—as someone you should fear and not cross in any way, shape, or form.

As Billy strolled to the plate, Dennis and Doug began to egg me on to yell at him while he was batting. I knew enough of Billy's reputation to know that this would not be in my best interest and I naturally said, "No way!"

At about this time, the manager of my brother's team strolled to the mound to have a conversation with his pitcher. I could only speculate, but I'm guessing he told his hurler to be careful with this batter because he could tie the game in one swing. Unfortunately for me, this gave my buddies more time to apply pressure to me.

"We dare you to yell at him. C'mon, Dave," they cajoled. "Don't be a chicken!" As kids, this was always the trump card when you wanted someone to do something that he didn't want to do. And here were my friends, throwing down the gauntlet with the "chicken" line. Still, I didn't bite. But then, they both put their thumbs under their armpits and began to flap their arms like chickens.

"Bwok, bwok, bwok!" they squawked as they strutted around, thrusting their heads forward and backward as they mocked me. Back then, I don't think it ever occurred to any of us that neither of them were willing to put their chicken necks on the line either. I, and only I, was facing the proverbial butcher's knife.

As my memory recounts, any time there were three boys playing together, inevitably a brouhaha would break out and it would be two against one. Sometimes you were in the two; sometimes you were the one. This time I was most definitely the one.

As the manager began to walk back to the dugout—which was really just a couple of benches behind the fence with no top or back to it—one of my friends pulled out the secret weapon. I don't remember which one said the words, but it was the final straw.

"Dave, we double-dog dare you to yell at him!"

It was as though time had stopped. Because when I was a kid, the double-dog dare was serious stuff. It's one thing to be called a chicken. For some reason one could live with that. You can't, however, back down from the double-dog dare. Accordingly, the pressure was too much and I succumbed to their pleas.

As the first pitch headed toward the plate, I yelled as loudly as I could, "Swing, batter, swing!" Billy took a mighty rip and missed.

"Strike one!" yelled the umpire. Dennis and Doug punched me in the arm, whooping and hollering.

"Way to go, Dave!" they hollered. The umpire turned to look at us with a puzzled look on his face, no doubt wondering why we were acting so crazy. Next, Billy turned to see where the voice had come from, and our eyes connected.

Quickly I looked away, not wanting to make eye contact and, at the same time, hoping he might think it was someone else who had yelled at him and not me.

As the pitcher went into his windup again, the two instigators pushed me for more.

"Swing, batter, swing!" I yelled again. Sure, I knew his name, I but was too afraid to say it out loud. Billy swung with the authority of Babe Ruth himself, along with a desire and determination to tie the game with a home run. But … he missed again!

"Strike two!" bellowed the umpire.

Once again Billy slowly turned to give me a glare that let me know he didn't appreciate my words of "encouragement" in this critical moment. Now, my two cowardly friends, who haven't said a word during Billy's turn at the plate, are *beside themselves* with excitement. They plead with me to keep it up for one more pitch.

After two strikes and two eye-piercing scowls, I'm feeling empowered. I'm feeling like I've had an impact on the game. One more strike and Phil's team walks off the field as winners and surely I will have played the most important role in making that happen!

"One more time, Dave, one more time," my friends urged me on. As the third pitch is hurled toward home plate, I summoned the courage from deep inside me.

"Swing, Billy, swing!" I heard myself screaming like a crazed fan at the World Series. Billy swings as if that same World Series is on the line.

"Strike three!" shrieked the umpire, at the same time raising his right hand toward the sky to signify the end of the game.

Dennis, Doug, and I jumped up and down and punched each other in the arms; high fives hadn't been invented yet. The victory was secure and we—no, I—had played a part! As we turned to walk away, I suddenly found myself face to face with Billy. In my rejoicing, I'd sort of forgotten about the big bully. Apparently, he felt I had something to do with the outcome of his last at-bat.

As we stood face to face—actually more eyes to chin—I looked down and saw him begin to clench his right fist. I knew what was coming, but was frozen like a statue. Billy rared back and punched me right in the stomach. Immediately, I doubled over in reaction to the blow. It only took a second to realize something else was going on. Billy had actually caught me a little lower than my stomach and hit me right in the bladder—and made me wet my pants!

As we walked home that evening, I can still remember the warm feeling I had—not because I had wet my pants, but because I had had the courage to do something that Dennis and Doug wouldn't do. Did it cost me something? Yes. Was it worth the pain and embarrassment? Yes, it was, to my six-year-old way of thinking.

When you stop and think about it, we all have opportunities to be cowardly or courageous almost every day! Both carry a price. But at the end of the day, which would you rather be—cowardly or courageous?

He who has overcome his fears will truly be free.

ARISTOTLE

Why Fear?

It's important to recognize that fear is a good thing. If you are sitting in your family room watching television and you smell something burning, it's a good idea to get up and check it out. If your house is on fire, gather up your family and get out. *Rational fear* is built into us to protect us and keep us from harm.

Irrational fear, on the other hand, keeps people from living life to the fullest. It keeps people from reaching their dreams. It keeps people from inventing things that might cure cancer or create a new mode of transportation.

I read somewhere once that, supposedly, Thomas Edison tried ten thousand times before he invented the light bulb. I've got to believe that after about ten tries someone was telling him, "Give it up, Tom. You're never going to make whatever it is you are trying to make." Still, he continued, and after about a thousand tries, I'd venture to say that people were talking about Tom the way they talked about Noah and his "stupid idea"—behind his back and, most likely, to his face as well.

Most people have some form of irrational fear. Maybe it's a fear of snakes or a fear of flying or a fear of crossing bridges (one of my fears). In some cases this is nothing more than a pebble-in-your-shoe fear. The fear is not great enough to change your life; it merely causes you some anxiety that makes life a little more difficult at times.

As I just admitted, I have a fear of crossing bridges. It doesn't matter if I'm walking, riding a bike, or driving a car. Whenever I cross a bridge, I have a twinge of anxiety that the bridge will collapse. I remember as a young boy riding in the car with my parents. I have no recollection of where we were going but we headed out of town and would cross over a small wooden bridge. That bridge would rumble and rattle as we crossed it and I was sure it was going to give way and we would end up in the river.

I used to manage a sales rep in the east bay of the San Francisco area. I would fly into the airport at the south end of "Frisco," and would need to cross the Bay Bridge further south to get to my destination. That bridge was about eleven miles long. Every time I crossed that bridge, I would diligently pray that there wouldn't be an earthquake.

It sounds pretty serious, but that fear was nothing more than a pebble-in-my-shoe fear. I have never not gone somewhere because I had to cross a bridge. I have never changed my route to get somewhere to avoid a bridge. I always take the quickest route, even if I have to cross a bridge or two. It merely causes me some anxiety, but it doesn't change my life.

The counter to the pebble-in-your-shoe fear is the boulder-in-your-path fear. This is fear that changes your life and causes you to take a different route to get to your destination.

In many cases, it even causes you to reach a different destination altogether.

This is the fear that keeps people from becoming who they were created to be. This is the fear that people don't like to talk about. It's the fear that is, at first glance, easy to avoid. People with a "boulder" fear seemingly always have a sense of being unfulfilled. They feel they have not tapped into their full potential, but facing their boulder is, more often than not, too scary to attempt—so they live in their fear, and usually with a great deal of frustration.

I know this because I am one of those people. I know because I have visited with enough people who feel the same way I do. I know because I have people who have started to talk with me about their fears and I began to challenge them to face their boulders. Oftentimes people simply avoid the "fear" guy because they don't want to go there, wherever "there" may be for them.

As I have visited with people, I asked them about their dreams. In many cases they would say, "Oh, it's really stupid," or "I could never do this, but I would like to ... " The dreams range from being a painter, to writing a book, to opening a bed and breakfast. When asked why they're not pursuing, or at least planning to pursue their dreams, the response usually centers around fear. The fears range from being afraid of what other people will think, to fear of losing their life's savings, to worry that it might not be the right time of life to go after their dreams. It may not come across as a fear, but when you dig deeper, it's definitely there, and there is no question—it's fear.

The Value of a Crisis

You can choose courage or you can choose comfort, but you can't choose both.

DR. BRENÉ BROWN

Chapter 3

Never Underestimate the Value of a Crisis

January 15, 2010, is a date I will never forget. I was informed I was being terminated from my position at a non-profit organization. The ranks of the unemployed were about to grow by one.

Anger and disappointment were my first reactions, but also a sense of relief as I had really been struggling in my role. My own fear had kept me working at a job that wasn't anything like I thought it would be when I took it, and one that never came close to meeting my expectations. Great people, lousy organization for me. Maybe you've been there.

As I began to process this dramatic life change, I thought to myself, "I'm a pretty sharp guy with some skills. I'll be able to find a job in a month or two." I didn't realize then how challenging it would be to find a job. At the same time, one of the greatest things I learned in losing my job is to never underestimate the value of a crisis. Courage is critical during times of crises in our lives.

Losing your job brings many potential ramifications that rise to the surface. My wife worked at our church, so her income was not one that we could exist on. In fact, she lost her job thirteen months after I lost mine.

We were now in a position where we might not be able to pay our bills and might even lose our house. This was a crisis in our lives. Thankfully, it wasn't like having a life-threatening illness or something similar, but in any case this crisis brought with it the great possibility of significant change in our lives.

So, where is the value in that? I'm glad you asked.

If I hadn't lost my job, and had instead continued to work, I never would have had to go down the path of introspection. While it hasn't been fun to relive and review the painful experiences that have happened in my life, it has truly been one of the most growing experiences in my life. God has shown Himself to me to be true in more ways than I could ever imagine.

If I had still been working, I would have continued to avoid thinking about my fears and then talking about them with others so they could, in turn, face their own fears. I could put on my happy face and let people think that Dave was one of those guys who had it all together. Great job, great family, great house. But the reality was, it was all a façade.

When you face a crisis, ask yourself, "What is God trying to teach me here? What can I learn and how can I make a difference for others through this?" Let me give you an example.

Jim Lovell was the captain of the "successful failure" Apollo 13 mission. Lovell was played by Tom Hanks in the 1995 award-winning film titled, simply, *Apollo 13*[1]. In the

1 Apollo 13. Hollywood, CA: Universal Pictures, 1995. Film.

film, literally the entire world watched as the injured space-craft made its way back to earth. As the craft goes through one harrowing experience after another on its return, the astronauts' families are shown in their homes watching the distressing scenes as they unfolded on national television. As Lovell's family watched the coverage, it switched to an old interview of Lovell as he talked about what it's like to be an astronaut. ABC TV science editor, Jules Bergman, asked Lovell, "Was there ever a specific instance in an airplane emergency when you recall fear in the cockpit?"

Lovell responded, "I remember this one time when I'm in a Banshee in combat conditions, so there were no running lights on the carrier. It was the Shangri-La." (A Banshee was a McDonnell F2H single-seat carrier-based jet and the USS Shangri-La was an aircraft carrier that was home to 90 to 100 jets.)

Lovell continued, "We were in the Sea of Japan, my radar had jammed, and my homing signal was gone ... because somebody in Japan was actually using the same frequency. And so it was ... leading me away from where I was sup-posed to be. And I'm looking down at a big, black ocean, so I flip on my map light and then suddenly, zap! Everything shorts out right there in my cockpit. All my instruments are gone. My lights are gone. I can't even tell now what my altitude is. I know I'm running out of fuel so I'm think-ing about ditching in the ocean. And I look down there and then, in the darkness, there's this green trail. It's like a long carpet that's just laid out right beneath me. And it was the algae, right? It was that phosphorescent stuff that gets churned up in the wake of a big ship and it was … it was just leading me home. You know? If my cockpit lights hadn't shorted out, there's no way I'd have ever been able to see that. So, uh … you never know what events are going to transpire to get you home."

Lovell lost everything except control of the plane, and even that control was short-lived. Crisis was at hand. Because he lost nearly everything, he was able to see what he needed to see and he safely landed on the Shangri-La.

Name Your Fear

Fear loses power when it's brought into the light.

DAVE CORNELL

Chapter 4

Name Your Fear

I was sitting in Mr. Wilson's ninth-grade algebra class. It was the third period of the day and my desk was on the north side of the room along a wall that was all windows. If there were people playing tennis, I had a great view of their match. Math was never a strong suit of mine, so I was as likely to be looking out the window as I was to be paying attention.

There was a rattling knock on the glass-paneled classroom door and immediately I knew. My dad was dead. Mom had awakened us the night before and told us that Dad was sick and the ambulance was coming to pick him up and take him to the hospital. She said she didn't know how serious it was and that we should get up in the morning and get ourselves off to school.

My dad was a pastor. Many nights he had meetings at church and so we often didn't see him in the evenings. We lived in a parsonage, literally ten steps away from the church through the back door. Often Dad would come home during a break to say hi and see how things were going and just visit with us. The night before was no different. He had a break and he came home and asked me where my goofy hat was. He wanted to provide some levity at his meeting and was going to wear this hat I'd made that resembled a dunce cap with a pointy top. That was the last time I saw him or talked to him.

Mr. Wilson opened the door to see who was interrupting his class. He quickly turned and said my name, "David, they need to see you in the office." As I got up, somehow knowing why I was being called to the office, my friends started saying things like, "What did you do now? Dave's in trouble!" and other comments friends make when one of the gang gets called to the office. I vividly remember thinking, "If they only knew why I was going to the office, they wouldn't be saying these things."

When I got to the office, I saw my older brother, Phil. He was a junior and had arrived at the office before I did. Father Reynolds, the priest from the local Catholic church, was also there standing next to Phil. He had either volunteered or been asked to come and get us out of school and take us home. He quickly told me that my dad had passed away. The school that Phil and I attended was a combination junior/senior high in the same building. We now needed to walk across the street to the lone elementary school in town to get my younger brother, Tom, who was in the fourth grade.

We had moved to Buffalo, Minnesota, when I was in the third grade. I can remember seeing our house and church for the first time. Since they were right next to each other, Dad certainly didn't have much of a commute to get to work! We always had breakfast together as a family, Dad would often come home for lunch, and we tried to eat dinner together every night as well. As I stood in the living room of our new parsonage home, I could look out the window and see the junior/senior high school right across the street. Since the church was right next to the parsonage, and on the other side of the church was the elementary school, everything that was important to my growing and maturing was less than a two-minute walk from my home.

On this day, Father Reynolds led us out of the elementary school for the short walk home. We stopped at the end of the wide sidewalk in front of the school. Father Reynolds faced the three of us and began talking. I don't remember what he said exactly but it went something like this: "Boys, your father has passed away. This is going to be a very difficult time for all of you, but especially for your mother. You now each need to become the man of the house in your own way. You need to do everything you can to help your mother get through this. You need to be strong, be men, don't cry, and don't ask any questions."

From there, we walked home from school in silence. When we walked through the back door into the kitchen, Mom was there waiting for us. I don't remember much about what was said, but after just a few moments Mom broke into tears and sat down on a little step stool, saying tearfully, "What are we going to do?"

I remember very little about the days surrounding my father's death and his funeral. There are bits and pieces of memories but, for the most part, it has been tucked deeply into the recesses of my mind somewhere. I spoke with a counselor once about that time in my life. He said that I had been through something very traumatic, though I'd never thought of it as trauma. He referred back to Father Reynolds' admonition for us not to cry. He said that when you suppress one emotion, you affect all of the emotions. Our emotions are not marked with a button that you push to manipulate them one way or another. In my case, by making sure I didn't cry I was, basically, shutting down all of my emotions. I have often felt flatlined through much of my life. I never got too high or too low. Some of that is my personality, but I believe that my mostly "even keel" was greatly brought about by my dad's death.

About three weeks after Dad died, basketball season started. Sports was always a big part of my life but I didn't realize the role that sports, in particular basketball, was about to play in my life. It was a Monday and I went home after my first practice. Supper was ready and Mom called us to the table. As we sat down, Mom realized she had set five places instead of four. She had set a place for Dad. She very calmly picked up the extra plate and took it back to the cupboard, commenting as she did so, "I can't believe I set five places." Immediately, she broke into tears and went back into her bedroom.

I don't remember how long she was back there or if any of us did anything. I just remember that the next night I didn't want to be home for supper. When practice was over, I simply stayed in the gym and shot baskets for a while. I then took my time getting showered and walked the short distance home when I thought supper would be done. Sure enough, when I got home supper was done and everyone had gone their separate ways. My meal had been neatly wrapped in foil and put in the refrigerator. I took it out, warmed it up in the oven and ate my supper in front of the TV. That seemed to work pretty well that night, so that's what I did every night after that—a very easy, convenient, painless way to avoid dealing with reality. We lived in that parsonage for seven more months. I never again ate supper at that kitchen table at the same time as my family.

Basketball became a place of refuge for me. The fact that I'm 6'7" and enjoyed it helped, but the game was a place where I could go and forget about life. Both in high school and college, I can remember coming out of the locker room after games and my teammates being met by their moms and dads. The reality of life smacked me in the face after every game. Mom was there and always incredibly supportive, but I was always different from everyone else. I watched as my teammates' dads looked at their sons after a big win. They beamed with pride and would give them a hug or put a hand on their sons' shoulders and say, "Great game, Son!"

It was November of 1969 when my dad died. Back in those days, you didn't seek help for traumatic experiences in life—at least we didn't. You simply manned up and moved on. There was never any talk of seeing a counselor. I don't remember anyone asking me how I was doing or if I needed any help. People may have done that, but if so, I simply don't remember. Many years later, Mom told me about how she asked me several times if I wanted to talk about what happened with Dad's death. She said I would just say no, that it hurt too much and I didn't want to talk about it. I don't remember any of those conversations but I'm sure they happened. Mom did the very best she could, considering the circumstances.

I often tell people that my mom was my hero. I don't have any idea how she was able to do what she did. When Dad died, she was a stay-at-home mom. Dad had a very small insurance policy that didn't cover much other than his funeral so the bottom line was, Mom had to go back to work. She had graduated from college with a degree in English but with no teaching certificate. She had planned on being a missionary to Africa when she met my dad. He had heard from a friend that she was going to Africa, so Dad knew he needed to act fast. He asked her to marry him on their first date.

Mom attempted to go back to school to get her teaching certificate, but it was just too much. She was trying to commute over an hour each way every day while raising three boys who were simply lost. She was still lost herself, and never had much chance to grieve because she had to take care of us. She eventually ended up getting a job as a study hall supervisor in the high school.

Since we lived in a parsonage, we also had to find another place to live. Somehow, Mom was able to buy a small house. I don't know this to be fact, but I believe that there were some members of the church who may have helped Mom to finance this house. Moving from the parsonage to our new home was another opportunity for me to avoid life. We made the move on Saturday, May 2, 1970. I told Mom that I had golf practice for the school golf team and needed to be there for it. We actually did have practice, though I probably could have gotten out of it, but I just didn't want to be there for the move. I got up and left the parsonage before the move started and simply came home to our new home after all the work was done.

As I reflect on my life, I believe the incident with Mom at the dinner table had a profound effect on how I dealt with, or didn't deal with, other issues that came up in my life. I recognize, now, how often I have simply found a way to avoid facing life and the challenges that are a part of life. I now understand that it's a form of fear. I also am now beginning to understand just how powerful fear has been in my life and in the lives of others.

After losing my job in 2010, someone told me about a four-part workshop designed to help people looking for work in, at best, a very difficult job market. I had been invited to join a group of three other guys, who were also without work, to attend the workshop together. When I got to the workshop, it felt like I was simply going through the motions. I knew the job market was tough, but I really didn't want to be there.

We were all given a workbook as part of the workshop.

During the first session we were assigned some homework: to write down our dream jobs, what we were passionate about, and what our fears were.

Which brings me to my dreams. What was it that I wanted to do that I avoided or ran from? When I was a boy, I wanted to be a pro athlete in whatever sport happened to be in season. I was going to be the next Harmon Killebrew or Fran Tarkenton or Bill Russell. When my dad died, I think I lost a lot of my dreams. Dad used to play catch or throw the football or shoot baskets with me. When he died, that all went away. My brothers were not into sports and had their own interests, so we all led pretty separate lives as kids.

As an adult, I knew what my dream job was, but I'd never written it down. I'd told a few people about it but to write it down was a different thing altogether—there was something more convicting about that. My passions tie into my dream job, so that wasn't as difficult because I was now into the exercise. Then came the hard part—my fears. That became an interesting and challenging exercise. I'd never really thought about my fears. Who wants to explore things that are uncomfortable? Deep down, I think I knew that I would have to explore how Dad's death had affected me and I didn't want to go there.

My dream job since I was about 28 years old was to be a professional motivational/inspirational speaker. I don't know why. I remember seeing one of these guys address an audience of high school students and teachers. He told some great stories and made some great points that even impacted me, and I wasn't the intended audience. I can remember thinking how cool that would be to stand up in front of an audience and make them laugh and inspire them at the same time.

After the speaker's presentation, I visited with him for a few minutes. I asked him how he got started and what one needed to do to become who he was. He said, "Find something you're passionate about and learn as much as you can. Develop stories around that passion and then find an audience." It seemed simple enough. But as I started to think about what I could be passionate about, I also started to think, "I could never do what he did." I didn't recognize it at the time, but fear was getting a hold on me.

While I had those beliefs, I also knew that whenever I had the chance to be in front of a group, I got energized. I greatly enjoyed teaching a Sunday school class or facilitating a discussion of work issues. In 1988, I went to work as a high school yearbook representative. I went through a very extensive training program and was really interested in the guys who were doing the training. I talked to them about how they got started in training. I was intrigued by teaching adults; by giving them information that would help them to do their jobs and even make a difference in their personal lives.

A year later, I was asked back to another sales class to give a presentation on what it was really like in the field as a sales rep. I remember preparing and trying to make my presentation informational, but fun and entertaining as well. I was nervous before I started but I quickly settled into my talk. What a rush I got as the talk went on! I hadn't had that much fun since playing basketball.

This experience made me start to think again about how cool it would be to make a living speaking to people. Apparently, I made a good-enough impression with the trainers that they asked me to become a part of the training team on occasion. I had the opportunity to watch and learn from people who had been doing this for years. They would tell me what worked and what didn't. I was able to put my personality into the portions of the training for which I was responsible. The feedback I got was amazing. It was always very positive and encouraging. It made me, again, want to explore this idea of speaking more. But I always heard this voice saying, "You could never do that," "You're not good enough," "Why would anyone want to listen to you?" I didn't recognize it at the time, but I now know that this was the voice of fear.

So I continued on my life's journey, working in the education sales field for twenty-two years. Periodically, I would have opportunities to speak and train. I even had a stretch for about three years when all I did was train. It was probably the most enjoyable time in my career. I was using my gifts and talents to help others discover who they were while helping them to become the very best they could become with their abilities. Whenever I had the chance to speak, I always wanted more. After I was finished, I couldn't wait for the next time. The feeling I got from speaking was identical to the feeling I had before, during, and after a basketball game in high school and college. It was a sense of great exhilaration and accomplishment.

On several occasions, I would feel so good about what I'd just experienced that I would begin to think about becoming a speaker again. I would come back and stand before my boulder. I knew the destination that I wanted to reach was on the other side of the boulder, and I badly wanted to get there, but I didn't know how. As I would think about becoming a speaker, the voice would return. "You can't do that." "Why would anyone want to listen to you?" "Who are you that you think you have anything to say that's of value?" I'd walk away from the boulder looking for a new destination. In my head, there was an actual picture of a boulder that stood in my path, preventing me from getting to where I wanted to go.

As I went through the fear exercise in the book, I spent a lot of time thinking about how my dad's death and the other events in my life all fit together. One of the fears that I have had most of my life is that I simply wouldn't live very long. I expected to die before I was 50. All of the men in my dad's family died early due to heart disease. The message, or the voice in my head, that I grew up with was that "Cornell men die young." So it isn't surprising that the belief that I developed as a result was that I would die young.

I have measured my life by the things that I have gotten to see in the lives of my kids that my dad never got to see: Confirmations, driver's licenses, high school graduations, college graduations. From babies to toddlers, to children, to teens, to adults—these were all milestones in life that my dad never got to see and, for some reason, I was blessed to get to see them all with my daughters. On September 19, 2009, I even got to walk my older daughter down the aisle at her wedding. That was a day that I never thought I would see. It was a surreal experience that was almost overwhelming and still brings tears to my eyes as I write about it.

Seeing grandchildren was also something I never thought much about. With my mindset, I presumed that I would never see that either. But on May 15, 2011, I was able to hold my granddaughter, Hallie Ruth. It was an overwhelming experience. There are not words to describe the feeling I had in holding her. It was, again, surreal—as though it was a scene in a movie because this wasn't supposed to happen to me.

Retirement was also something I never even considered. I would die long before retirement age. As a result, there was no need to plan for retirement. I wasn't frivolous with my money but I certainly didn't put any away for the future. Knowing I was going to die young, my plan was to have an insurance policy that would take care of my family when I was gone. It's not like I didn't have a plan, it just wasn't a very good one.

January 8, 2008, marked another kind of milestone, because on this date I had lived longer than my dad. I was aware of that date for long before it ever came around. It was not uncommon then, and still happens frequently now, that I would go to bed and wonder if I would wake up in the morning. As a Christian, I wasn't afraid of dying—in fact, I had prepared in many ways for it—but instead, I seemed to have a fear of living.

Fear is a manipulative emotion that can
trick us into leading a boring life.

DONALD MILLER

Chapter 5

Self-Talk

Understanding your self-talk is a critical piece to understanding your boulder of fear and being able to begin to
work through it. When I would come back and face my
boulder and consider trying, again, to become a speaker,
the voice would begin to speak. Here are some examples of
the things I would tell myself:

- "Who are you that anyone would want to hear what you
  have to say? You have no credibility with anyone. You're
  just a guy. There's nothing special about you."

- "There's nothing special about being able to stand up in
  front of a group and speak. *Anyone* can do that."
  I have always discounted the gifts that God has given
  me. Speaking is something that comes easily for me.
  I still get nervous but, as I mentioned before, I also
  am energized by it. Because it comes easily, I make an
  assumption that it comes easy for everyone. I don't see
  that there is anything special about it. Anyone could do
  this.

- "If you were a good speaker, you would have people
  asking you to speak more often." Over the years,
  I've had chances to speak to a variety of groups and

I figured if I was any good, people who'd seen me would ask me back to speak at other events or organizations.

- "You don't have any letters behind your name." I have an undergrad degree and three classes toward a master's. The only reason I started the program was to get the letters, which I thought would give me the credibility I needed to become a speaker.

- "You don't have a dramatic story." Whenever I would hear a speaker that I liked, I would go to his/ her website. More often than not, in my mind, these speakers had a dramatic story that attracted an audience. He survived an airline hijacking. She survived cancer. He was orphaned at the age of three and raised by wolves in the wilderness until the age of twelve! You get the idea.

- "Life happens *to* you." While this was not a recurring statement by my voice, it was a fact that I had assigned myself.

During one of the three graduate classes I took, I had to give a presentation as part of the class. At the end of the class that day, the professor asked me to stay afterward for a moment. She asked me why I was part of this master's program. I told her that I thought I needed to get the advanced degree to help me in my career. Earlier in the class we had done an assessment on our gifts and skills. We had to talk about our dreams and what we felt we were gifted to do. It was one of the few times that I talked about my desire to be a speaker, so the professor knew of my dream.

As I mentioned earlier, I'm 6'7" and she was only about 5'4". But she wasn't intimidated at all. She did one of those things where she took her index finger, poked me in the chest, and said, "You already have everything you need to accomplish your dream. You don't need any letters. By not pursuing your dream, you are denying God the pleasure that He created you for." Wow! No one had ever been that blunt with me before—or since. I don't know of anyone who wants to deny God the pleasure of what He created you for. I got the message, but still it took a long time for me to act on it.

The voice—the negative self talk—is a powerful influence in your battle against fear. You have to be willing to face the voice and find reasons why the voice isn't right or truthful.

For many, the voice of negative self-talk is similar to a default setting on a computer. Your mind automatically goes negative because it has done it for so long. We get so accustomed to the default that we don't recognize the impact it has on our daily lives. We need to become aware of our default setting in order to begin to change it.

Name-Your-Fear Action Steps
1. Write down your fears.
- Many of our fears eat us up on the inside. It's important to get them out on paper and, in a sense, release them to be dealt with. The more familiar you are with what's holding you back, the easier it will be to deal with it. Writing down your fears takes away some of their power.

- Write down what your fear is costing you. You are likely paying a price in several ways: emotionally and physically as well as a dollar cost.

- Begin to write scenarios in which you have overcome your fear and what that looks like in your life.

2. Write down your self-talk.

- Just as you did by writing down your fear, writing down your self-talk takes its power away. As I mentioned earlier, our self-talk is often a default. We need to have an awareness of how often it affects us so that we can change it. That's what writing it down does.

3. Find a mentor and a cheerleader.

- Most people who are being controlled by fear do it in private. We need to have people in our lives who walk alongside us, encourage us, and challenge us in overcoming our fear. Don't hide alone in your fear. Share it with someone and let them help you.

Frame Your Fear

Everything you've ever wanted
is on the other side of fear.

JACK CANFIELD

Chapter 6

Frame Your Fear

Fear can have a powerful hold on our lives and dreams. During my journey, I recognized that I had to see my fear differently if I wanted to overcome it.

When I was in the second grade, my teacher, Miss Vybral, called my parents and told them she thought I was having vision problems. She said I was squinting from my seat in my effort to see things on the chalkboard.

My mom promptly made an appointment for me with the optometrist in Wahoo. I was told I had fairly significant astigmatism and glasses would be the appropriate remedy. Back in those days, it took a week to ten days before you got your glasses because they had to send the prescription out to a lab to have them made and then shipped back.

When they arrived, I went with my mom after school and picked them up. Let it be known that I did not want to be a guy with glasses. I personally had been known to call kids "four eyes" if they were bespectacled. Upon arriving home, I wore the glasses all evening until I went to bed. When I got up, I put them on and wore them while I got ready for school and had breakfast. However, when I walked out the back door to go to school, my glasses did not stay on for very long. When I left for school, I would walk down an alley behind our house. At the street where the alley ended, I would make a right-hand turn on the sidewalk. After reaching this point, there was a hedge, and I knew that Mom could no longer see me. There I would immediately take my glasses off and put them in my pocket. When school was over, just before I reached the alley, I would take them out of my pocket and put them back on.

When you're seven years old, you don't think too far into the future. I never thought about my parents finding out about my little ploy which, in my mind, was foolproof. But, they did. At some point, my teacher called my mom and said that I was continuing to squint. Mom explained to her that we had gone to the eye doctor and that I had gotten glasses.

"He's not wearing them," Miss Vybral told my mom.

I remember having the inevitable little sit-down chat with Mom and Dad about needing to wear my glasses, and how it was hurting me, and how much money they had spent on the glasses. The strange thing is, and I have no recollection of how this happened, but somehow I ended up not having to wear my glasses.

When I was about twenty four, I was working for a small radio station in western Colorado. One of my roles was to do play-by-play for several of the area high school athletic teams. We covered football, basketball, volleyball, wrestling, baseball, and even summer city-league softball games.

When I went to cover my very first event, a high school

football game, I found out just how bad my vision had become. Following the opening kickoff, the team I was covering was marching toward the goal line. I was in my broadcaster's perch at about the fifty-yard line at the top of the bleachers. As they moved down the field to the 30, then the 25, and then the 20, I realized I couldn't make out the great big numbers on the backs of the players' jerseys. It was my responsibility to tell people what was going on, and my vision kept me from doing my job.

Over the years, I had somehow adapted to my impaired vision. I had deceived myself into believing that I could see better than I really could. But I knew I had to see differently in order to do my job. This time, I went to the eye doctor on my own. He stated in no uncertain terms that the vision in my left eye was horrible and basically the right eye was doing all the work. He explained that I was going to get glasses that would be very strong and that it would take some time to get used to wearing them. He even said that I might get physically ill if I wore the glasses too long at one time, recommending that I wear them for only five to ten minutes at a time until I adjusted to them.

He was right. Wow, were they strong. I remember putting them on for the first time and getting dizzy after just a couple of minutes. It took about a week before I was able to wear them full time. But I was amazed at how clear my vision was with my new glasses! What had I missed in all of those years without them? It was a whole new world for me.

Our fears are much the same way. We have dreams and

visions of things we want to do or accomplish in our lives, but our fear keeps us from pursuing them. We adapt and deceive ourselves into thinking that it's okay, that someday we'll go after the dream, whatever the dream might happen to be.

Something that has helped me in my journey is to "FRAME" my fear. The FRAME is a tool that helped me begin to see and view my fears differently. I learned the FRAME principles from a group called Top 20 Training. The organization works primarily with students to help them see the world they live in differently so they can begin to make better, positive choices that will have a positive outcome on their lives. These same principles that work for students will work in overcoming your fears as well. The FRAME is shown in the diagram below.

THE FRAME

What the Frame suggests is the following:

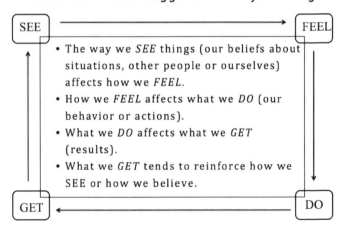

- The way we *SEE* things (our beliefs about situations, other people or ourselves) affects how we *FEEL.*
- How we *FEEL* affects what we *DO* (our behavior or actions).
- What we *DO* affects what we *GET* (results).
- What we *GET* tends to reinforce how we SEE or how we believe.

To understand the FRAME, you simply start in the upper left-hand corner and follow the arrows around the frame. How we see things affects how we feel about them, which in turn causes us to take certain actions, which will get us a certain result, which returns us to how we saw something in the first place. In essence, it is self-fulfilling prophecy.

If we see ourselves as having very little control over our lives, we will feel lost and adrift. We will do very little to change our situations because we have no control, which will get or keep us in a state of despair that leads us to say, "See, I told you I don't have any control over what happens to me!"

The FRAME encourages us to change how or what we *SEE* to get a different result. If we can begin to see that perhaps we have at least some control over our lives, then maybe we will take some small steps to prove that's the case, which will get us a different and better result.

As I so often explored the idea of owning my own business as a speaker and a coach, I would see my fear being in control of me, instead of *me* being in control of my fear. As a result, I continued to fail because I stayed in the same mindset, or the same *SEE*, about my ability to become a speaker. But my mindset began to change when I began to really see my fear in a whole new way.

Courage isn't having the strength to go on—
it is going on when you don't have the strength.

NAPOLEON BONAPARTE

Chapter 7

Fear is Selfish

When I was in the eighth grade, we had an exchange student who came to our school from Venezuela. His name was Steve Larson. I'm still trying to figure out how a guy from Venezuela was named Steve Larson!

I lived in what was, at the time, an all-white rural community. People were wearing their hair longer. Steve had darker skin, a very short haircut, and very thick glasses (like those I should have been wearing if I had listened to my parents!). No one, including me, paid any attention to Steve. He was different from the rest of us in so many ways that everyone just avoided getting to know him.

Steve's host family attended the church where my father was the pastor. One day his host mom asked my mom if I would be willing to spend a Saturday morning with Steve because he didn't have any friends and was really miserable and homesick. My mom said that I would love to do that and then came home and told me what I would love to do. Have you been there?

I tried to tell Mom that Steve was really weird and different and no one liked him. It didn't make any difference. Mom said I was going to spend the next Saturday morning with Steve. I never told any of my friends of my Saturday plans because I was afraid of what they would think.

When Saturday arrived, Mom drove me out to Steve's place. As you might guess, I had a great time. Steve was funny. He was athletic. He was a great guy. If my friends got to know Steve, they would think the same thing. I actually ended up calling my mom and asking if I could spend the whole day with him!

On Monday when I went to school, I gathered with my friends in our usual gathering spot. As we talked about what we had done over the weekend, I never mentioned a word about my Saturday with Steve. I was still too afraid my friends would laugh at me and say things I might not want to hear. After we had been talking for a few minutes, one of my friends saw Steve come into view. He said, loud enough for everyone to hear (including Steve), "Hey, there's Cokes!" This was one of the nicknames we had for Steve because of his thick glasses.

Everyone laughed, including me, and all eyes turned to Steve. He stopped in his tracks to see where the hurtful words had come from. Immediately, he saw me and we locked eyes. He waited for me to call him over, to defend him, to tell my friends that I had spent Saturday with him and how we'd had a great time.

I wish I could say that's what I did. But I didn't say a word. I just laughed along with everyone else. Steve stared at me for a second or two longer. Then he started to cry. He put his head down and shuffled away to his destination. I had been so afraid of what my friends would think that I didn't have the courage to stand up for Steve.

Fear is selfish.

Because of my fear, I denied Steve the chance to be a part of my group and to have great memories of our little town, rather than the miserable ones I'm sure he has. Because of my fear, I denied my friends the chance to get to know Steve and find out what a great guy he was.

So often, our irrational fears are about self-protection at the expense of others. Through this journey of fear and courage, I am learning to ask myself a powerful question when faced with the need be courageous. The question is this: Who pays the price for your fear? Steve paid a price that day. My friends paid a price that day. And I continue to pay a price because of my cowardice.

Let's look at another example on a much larger scale with a much larger price.

Back in 2011, the child molestation case of Jerry Sandusky, a longtime assistant football coach at Penn State University, came to light. In 2012, Sandusky was convicted on 45 of 48 counts of child sexual molestation.

www.nytimes.com/interactive/2012/07/12/sports/ncaa-football/13pennstate-document.html)

In the fall of 2000, two custodians on the same day witnessed Sandusky, on separate occasions with separate boys, molesting them. In the Freeh Report on page 65, they are referred to as Janitor A and Janitor B. They both met with

Janitor C, a senior custodian, to share with him what they saw. Janitor C told Janitor A what he needed to do was report what he had witnessed.

Janitor A stated to the other two in fearing for his job, "No, they'll get rid of all of us." The three custodians chose to stay in their fear rather than act courageously by reporting what they had seen.

Janitor B told the special investigator that reporting the incident, "... would have been like going against the President of the United States in my eyes. I know Paterno has so much power, if he wanted to get rid of someone, I would have been gone."

The sexual abuse went on for eleven more years before it finally ended when an assistant coach had the courage to talk about what he had seen. This young man did pay a price as he was vilified in the press and did lose his job. Over time, he has been vindicated and lauded for his courage.

Many more young boys and their families paid a huge mental, emotional, and physical price for those custodians not being willing to speak up.

There is a price to be paid for living in fear or living in courage. Often, we don't think about the cost of our decisions to stay in fear or to move forward into courage. Both will likely cost us something. Sometimes it's monetary. Sometimes it's relationships. Sometimes it's feelings of guilt or shame. Sometimes it's physical.

I paid a price when I was hit in the stomach by Billy after my brother's baseball game. It was worth it. Knowing the outcome, I'd pay that price again. For Jane, the escalator lady, her granddaughter was paying a price every time Jane steered her toward the stairs or the elevator. Jane was denying her granddaughter something she loved.

I truly believe the price for living in fear is much bigger than the price for living in courage. I often wonder how the three custodians deal with not having spoken up about what they saw. Could they have lost their jobs? Yes, they sure could have. I'm sure they would tell you today that it would have been worth losing their jobs if they knew then what they know now. That would have been a small price to pay compared to the price now being paid by the victims as well as these men for not speaking up.

Think about the fear you have in your life right now. Perhaps it's having a difficult conversation with a child. Maybe you need to let your top producer go because he is having such a negative impact on your whole organization. Maybe you've been wrestling with allowing your elderly parent to drive because you're afraid of his or her reaction to the conversation you know needs to happen.

Who is paying a price, or who might pay a price, because of your fear of having the conversation?

As I went on my journey of unemployment, looking for work, going through counseling, and thinking about starting a business as a speaker, I had an epiphany. I had created my presentation on fear and courage but it was still in its infancy stage. I liked the overall presentation, but it was still missing something.

I was fortunate to be asked to speak to several job networking groups to share my story. After every presentation, people told me in dramatic ways how my story had affected them and the difference it was making for them on their journey as they searched for work. What I hadn't expected was people telling me the difference it was making in their personal lives as well.

Whenever I would speak—and this continues to this day—as I was driving to the event, I would wonder why these people had asked me to speak. The voice, the negative self-talk I referenced earlier, would take over and the deep-seated fears would begin to raise their ugly heads. I wasn't worthy or adequate enough to be speaking to whatever audience it was that had asked me to speak. As I processed through this and visited with my counselor about it, I came to a revelation.

As a Christian, I believe we are born with gifts, talents, and abilities given to us by our Creator. These gifts are not for us, but they are to be used by us to make a difference for the people we encounter in our lives everyday. I have always struggled to accept as a gift my ability to speak and communicate. It comes so naturally for me and I get great joy out of doing it, so it's hard to see that as a gift. But, slowly, I am coming to the realization that my ability to tell stories that make a difference in the lives of others *is* a gift.

Another "gift" that I wish to embrace is my sense of humor. I must admit that I enjoy making others laugh. When I speak and train, I want people to have fun. I want them to learn, but I also want them to enjoy themselves.

Over the course of my adult life I have taught a variety of Sunday school classes. On the very first Sunday of one of the classes I taught, there was an elderly lady named Joyce who showed up and positioned herself right in the front row right in the middle chair. On that first day, I didn't know her name but I had seen her in church many, many times. I knew she was single but didn't know if she was widowed, divorced, or never married. Church was her community, and she was there every chance she got.

She was a tiny little woman who, quite literally, was about half my size. If she had gone to an amusement park, I'm sure she wouldn't have been tall enough for many of the rides. As the course progressed, she never said very much, but she certainly seemed to be enjoying herself. When we broke into small-group discussions, she participated greatly—but never in the big group. However, Joyce seemed to always have a smile on her face and she laughed often.

After about week six or seven, Joyce came up to me after class and said, "You make me laugh and you make me feel good. I learn a little bit, too, but I enjoy the class because you make me laugh and you make me feel good."

If I allow my fear to control my life, and don't speak and share my stories that will make a difference for others, that is incredibly selfish on my part. As you read early on, fear can be a boulder in your path that affects every area in your life. Fear doesn't require us to be courageous, but if we want to move the boulder, we have to begin to take courageous steps. We must exercise the courage muscle. The more often we do courageous things, the more courageous we get. What can you do today to begin moving your boulder?

In recognizing fear as being selfish, you need to begin to remove yourself from the equation. You need to stop thinking about how your fear will affect you and focus on how your fear is affecting others. By taking you (u) out of the equation in moving your boulder, you get *bolder*!

Frame-Your-Fear Action Steps

1. **Write down the messages that are holding you back.**
   Just as with the exercises Name Your Fear, writing down your messages will remove some of their power. Again, these thoughts are often defaults and we don't even recognize them. Be very aware of your messages.

2. **Write down your old "See" and what you want your new "See" to look like.**
   Begin to visualize a different way of doing things than you have in the past.

3. **Write down who is paying a price for your fear.**
   As you can tell, writing down things is one of the most powerful ways to courageously work through your fears. Who are the people whose lives will be different if you become a person of courage? How will your life, and how will their lives, be different if you act with courage?

Claim Your Courage

Fear calls us to be spectators.
Courage calls us to get in the game.

DAVE CORNELL

Chapter 8

Claim Your Courage

When my wife and I moved out of the home we had lived in for fifteen years, we purged a lot of stuff that we had gathered over time. One of the things I did was clean out a drawer in a filing cabinet I had in my office. The bottom drawer was full of personal files that had accumulated over the years.

As I went through that bottom drawer, I found ten separate file folders dating as far back as 1987. Each file detailed a time when I had tried to start a speaking business. *Ten times before,* I had faced my boulder! I had pushed and pushed that boulder in an effort to move it and make my living as a speaker. And each time I had turned away while my dream went back into the drawer for another day.

Now it was time to face the boulder and do something different.

I'd always had this vision in my head of a boulder that was blocking my path. It was as though the boulder was physically in the road on the way to my future, and I couldn't get around it. So I did some simple Internet research on how boulders are moved when they come off a mountain or a hill and close a road. It turns out, there are no machines or pieces of equipment that are large enough to move some of those giant boulders that end up blocking traffic on roadways.

Instead, the process of removing them is similar to the process I had to go through to fulfill my dream of running my own speaking business. First, experts are brought in to best determine how to break down the boulder into manageable pieces. They use jackhammers and dynamite and everything possible to break one giant boulder into thousands of little pieces that can be scooped up and hauled away. Next, the crews look for cracks and crevices where the breakdown process will begin. It takes a lot of time and hard, tiring, painstaking work.

The same is true in courageously working through your fears—to get to the other side of your boulder. I realized that I could no longer try and move the boulder in one big chunk. I had to break it down into manageable pieces, just as the road crews had to do.

During my time of unemployment, I went through intense counseling. I was diagnosed with situational depression. I often didn't want to get out of bed in the morning. I wasted countless hours watching TV, surfing the Internet, or simply sleeping while I tried to figure out what I was going to do. Through my counseling, I discovered how much control my negative voices and thoughts had over me.

I began to write down what I was telling myself when I thought about what I wanted to do. I became very conscious of how often those voices spoke to me and how they affected my mood and my ability to move toward my goal.

Becoming aware of the things I was telling myself became an incredibly powerful step toward changing the negative patterns that had developed, not just in my unemployment, but, really, during the course of my life.

When you have an awareness of your negative voice, you create an opportunity to do something about it. Before, when the negativity came, I didn't even recognize it and just let it drive my thoughts and my actions. Now, the awareness allowed me to take a different path.

With the help of my counselor, I came up with a strategy to deal effectively with the negative voices whenever they spoke up. I'll give you some examples from my list, but your steps may be completely different based on your situation and what is comfortable for you.

The first thing I did when I recognized the negative self-talk was to pray. As I Christian, I simply asked that God would take away those thoughts and replace them with affirming words that would help me move forward.

Next, I was encouraged to simply be grateful. In spite of what I didn't have any longer, I still had more than so many people throughout the world. It's amazing how looking at the world with eyes of gratitude changes your perspective on so many things. As I began to be more grateful, I also seemed to become so much more aware of the people around me and the different challenges they were facing. As I thought about the life-changing and potentially life-ending situations facing people I knew, at least on a more than casual level, I realized I would never want to trade places with them.

A third action step I took was to read books that I found challenging and encouraging. There were several, but here are a few I highly recommend: *Daring Greatly* by Dr. Brené Brown, *Telling Yourself the Truth* by Dr. William Backus, and *A Million Miles in a Thousand Years* by Donald Miller. There were more as well, but it is important for you to seek out books and authors that fit you and your situation.

You can never cross the ocean until you
have the courage to lose sight of the shore.

CHRISTOPHER COLUMBUS

Chapter 9

The Lesson of the Crack

Now, if you're like me and still have a bit of junior-high boy in you, let me assure you that there is far more to this than you might initially think. Have you ever seen a tree seemingly growing out of a rock? How in the world does that happen?

The reality is, that tree or plant or whatever isn't really growing out of the rock. That seed found a crack in the rock in which to grow. The seed is rooted in the soil and slowly finds its way through something we would never think possible. It also finds the sunlight and the rain it needs to have life!

The very same principle is true for us as humans in the challenges we face. We need to be resilient enough to find the cracks in our boulders, and battle through the challenges until we find the light that draws us to a whole new life!

As it happened, the "crack" for me in my journey was the word "maybe." Early in this journey, I had the opportunity to meet and do some work with an organization discussed earlier called Top 20 Training, a group that helps school kids to develop strong character and a positive mindset.

In one of their courses, Top 20 Training introduces the importance of the word *maybe* in working through the cracks in your boulder. If I always wanted to be a speaker but never felt I was good enough, or that anyone would want to listen to me, my negative mindset would bring about thoughts like, "I could never be a speaker." In the Top 20 mindset, simply adding the word *maybe* to the front of that statement creates a crack in that old mindset (boulder) that opens up a whole new world of possibility.

"Maybe I could never be a speaker." This statement lets in a little sliver of hope and the possibility that "maybe I could be a speaker." So what are the things that you tell yourself you can't do? What happens if you simply put the word "maybe" in front of that negative, definitive statement that is derived from a negative mindset?

Suddenly, you begin to recognize opportunity. You begin to chip away at that great big boulder and get the energy to break it down into workable pieces. This one simple word –maybe—gives you both courage and optimism.

A great example of being able to see the crack comes from the timeless comedy *Dumb and Dumber*. If you've seen the movie, you'll recognize the scene immediately.

Lloyd is one of the lead characters, played by Jim Carrey. Jim and his good friend, Harry, have found a suitcase full of money. Lloyd and Harry do not score very high on the intelligence scale.

The plot of the movie is Lloyd and Harry doing their best, which isn't very good, to return the loot to its rightful owners. During their escapades, they become acquainted with an attractive woman with whom Lloyd becomes instantly smitten.

Lloyd now has two quests. First, to return the money, but second, and maybe, most important to Lloyd, to begin a relationship with the beautiful Mary Swanson.

Lloyd and Mary finally meet. This is Lloyd's chance to express his affection to Mary. He begins by asking her this question, "What do you think the chances are of a guy like you and a girl like me ending up together?"

Mary, wanting to be kind and to let him down easy replies, "Not good."

Lloyd needed more information so he asks, "You mean not good like one out of a hundred?"

Mary hesitantly but confidently says, "I'd say more like one out of a million."

Lloyd sees the crack. He sees the opportunity even though it is incredibly small. With a big smile on his face and possibility in his eyes, Lloyd says to Mary just as confidently as she did to him, "So you're tellin' me there's a chance!"

Can you courageously find the crack in your boulder?

Courage is resistance to fear, mastery of fear—
not absence of fear.

MARK TWAIN

Chapter 10

Chipping Away at the Boulder

Now that you have a sliver of hope because of the word *maybe*, it's time to begin to chip away at your boulder. Here are some ideas to help you begin to do that. This is the list I created for myself during my unemployment journey. Your list might look very different from mine, but it can be a road map to get you started.

- **Recognize that fear will always be there.**
  So often people wait for the fear to subside or go away before they do anything to improve themselves or go after their dreams. If you wait for the fear to dissipate or disappear, you will never start. Courage is about moving forward *in spite of* your fear. The fear will never be gone, but your courage needs to be bigger than your fear.

- **Stop going around the boulder.**
  When I found ten separate files cataloging the times I had either thought about starting, or actually did attempt to start a speaking business, I had determined the boulder was simply too big to move and so I walked away. But the last time, I stayed. I figured out I needed to break down the boulder and get it into workable pieces that I could simply scoop up and throw away.

There is no substitute for the hard work it takes to break down the boulder. Just do it!

- **Do something scary every week.**
Remember, courage is like a muscle. The more you work it, the stronger it gets. The more you face your fears, the more courageous you become. Learn to get comfortable being uncomfortable! This can be anything from going out and singing karaoke, to participating in a triathlon, to volunteering in a prison. It doesn't matter. Begin to do scary things so you can see that being scared is okay, and most of the time you come out unscathed!

- **Celebrate small victories.**
We often forget about the small steps it takes to get where we want to go or to fulfill our dreams. The ancient Chinese philosopher, Lao Tzu, said, "The journey of a thousand miles begins with a single step." When I started to write this book, I did a little happy dance celebration in my mind—simply because I started it! Those little celebrations keep us going and keep us taking the next step toward our goals or our dreams.

- **See failure as an opportunity and not an ending.**
Tying into the last point is recognizing that our failures help us learn. All too often, when I failed in my own life, I simply stopped trying rather than recognizing the effort and the learning that came as a result of the failure.

- **Don't discount your own abilities.**
When I was a sophomore in high school, I was brought

up to be a part of the varsity basketball team. This was a pretty big deal in my small Minnesota town. I believe we are all far more capable than that for which we give ourselves credit.

- **Get in the game!**
  Far too many people live a life that is reactive rather than proactive. They wait for something good to happen for them and then when it doesn't, they wonder why everyone else always gets the breaks. If you are one of those people, let me tell you very simply that it's time to get in the game. Stop waiting and start doing!

I'm going to expand on these last two bullets by relating a story. As a high-school sophomore, I still played on the junior varsity team, but my coach told me that I would dress for the varsity games and that he would put me in if we were way ahead or way behind to help me get experience for my junior and senior years.

In high school, you had a pretty good idea of which teams were the good ones and which ones weren't so good. I always had a pretty good idea of which games I might get to play in for the varsity game. I sat on the end of the bench and next to me was my friend, Steve. Steve and I were always the last two guys into the game when we were way ahead or behind. Steve usually went in first because of his junior status and I last because of my lowly sophomore ranking.

When there was a game in which Steve and I knew we wouldn't play, Steve came up with a brilliant idea. Because we were simply going to be fans and not get in the game, Steve thought it would be a good idea to give the manager some money and ask him to get us pop and popcorn so we could enjoy the game just as a fan would. The manager agreed and each game, he placed our refreshments underneath our seats so we could eat and watch. He even refreshed us at halftime!

Late in the season, we were playing one of our rivals. We were tied with them for the conference lead. There was no way I would play in this game. Steve and I had our snacks, as always. The game was very close, just as we expected. There were numerous ties and lead changes throughout the game. With about five minutes to go, the score was tied. I reached into my bag of popcorn and filled my mouth as I sat on the edge of my seat like any good fan during a close game. All of a sudden, I heard my name being called. "Cornell, Cornell!" I looked down toward the coach and he was waving me in his direction. I thought to myself, "What could he want? Maybe he wants towels or needs water, but why wouldn't he have the manager do that?"

I put down my popcorn and ran toward the coach to see what he needed. He simply said, "Get in the game for Davis!" With my mouth still full of popcorn, I headed to the scorers' table, pointed at my jersey, and went into the game for Davis. In the last five minutes of the game I scored five points, grabbed four rebounds, and blocked a shot. I wish I could tell you we won the game, but we didn't. The point is that I was far more capable to be in that situation than I believed myself to be. My coach saw things in me that I didn't see in myself. He had been watching me in practice and in B-squad games over the course of the entire season. He knew I had developed enough to be successful in that situation.

Often, just like my coach, people see things in us that we don't see in ourselves. What is it that you do in your life for which people give you glowing reviews and reports? Often, because it comes easily and naturally to you, you simply shrug it off as no big deal. *It is a big deal.* Listen to the people who encourage you and push you to use your gifts and talents!

When my coach waved me down to put me in the game, he didn't have a conversation with me. He didn't say, "Dave, the score is tied right now and I think this would be a good time to put you in the game. What do you think?" No! He simply said, "Get in the game."

Often, during the extended time of unemployment before starting my business, I would lie awake in bed and lament my lack of accomplishment of anything significant during that particular day. The regret of wasted time was incredibly heavy. On the other hand, when I had a particularly productive day, I would often lie in bed and feel good about what I had accomplished. I wouldn't beat myself up over wasted time and lack of production.

It takes courage to live a disciplined life. It's a lesson I am still learning, and there will always be room for growth.

Claim-Your-Courage Action Steps

1. Create your list to eliminate negative thoughts. Have a defined strategy to deal with the negative thoughts and self-talk you have.

2. Do something scary every week. Most of us live in a very comfortable world. Get comfortable with being uncomfortable. Ride a roller coaster. Sing karaoke. Go to a different restaurant. Strike up a conversation with a complete stranger.

3. Celebrate small victories. You won't overcome your fear in one giant leap. Celebrate the little things you do that get you one step closer to your courageous life.

Courage starts with showing up
and letting ourselves be seen.

DR. BRENÉ BROWN

Chapter 11

Closing Thoughts and An Old Zen Tale

Courage requires one to be active and not passive. Courage requires one to be uncomfortable. If you are too comfortable, most likely you aren't very courageous. It's also likely you are living a life of fear. To illustrate our boulder analogy, I would like to share a story that I once heard that is of unknown origin, but which paints a beautiful picture of courage and determination.

There once was a king of a medieval kingdom. It was a walled kingdom with only one gate. The king had no sons and needed to find a proper heir to take over the throne of his kingdom when he was gone. He sought counsel from his advisers and they came up with a plan after much discussion and conversation.

The king ordered his army to place a large boulder in the middle of the lone gate leading into the kingdom. Whoever had the courage to move the boulder would become the heir to the throne. By placing the boulder in the middle of the gateway, it kept people from taking their horses and chariots in and out of the kingdom. Travel and commerce with other kingdoms nearby were greatly impeded.

From his tower in the castle, the king could look directly down on the gate as the boulder was put in place. He had some ideas as to whom he thought would move the boulder. Some of the kingdom's finest men attempted to move the boulder shortly after it was placed in its inconvenient position. Without success, they walked away shaking their heads.

After several days, the king began to be discouraged as no one was even attempting to move the boulder anymore. Was there no one in the kingdom having the wherewithal to move the boulder and be the next king?

As time passed, people began to adapt to the boulder being in the middle of the gateway. They were able to walk around the boulder, and so they settled for life being more challenging because of its placement. After several months, the king had stopped keeping watch on the gate.

Then one day, one of the king's advisers called him to come to the tower. The king looked down in amazement. Pushing on the boulder was a man in tattered clothing. He was a peasant from the kingdom and he had been away for some time and was just returning to the area. He pushed and pushed and, like all the others, failed to move the boulder.

As the king watched the peasant walk away from the boulder, he, too, walked away from the tower, all hope vanished once again. The next morning, one of the king's men came and got him again. "Come quickly," he said to the king.

When the king looked down on the gateway, he saw the same peasant with some planks and stones and other tools. Slowly the man began to create fulcrums and to edge the boulder, ever so slowly, from the center of the gateway.

The peasant continued to work and, eventually, was able to move the boulder completely out of the gateway. Many had gathered over the long hours and watched the peasant work. When he was finished, they all cheered. The king smiled a great, royal smile. He sent two of his men to bring the lowly peasant into his presence.

As the man leaned against the boulder in exhaustion and satisfaction, he noticed a small indentation in the ground where the boulder had been. He walked over to the shallow hole and noticed a beautiful velvet bag lying on the ground. He picked it up, opened the bag, and looked inside. The bag was full of gold, silver, and jewels of many colors.

Just as he was looking into the bag, he was grabbed by the king's men, one on each arm. Scared that he was being mistaken for a thief, he pleaded with the men, "I didn't steal the bag. I simply found it on the ground where the boulder had been." The men said nothing and continued escorting him to the castle. They brought the man before the king, who was sitting on his throne.

The man fell face first on the floor. He tossed the bag of treasure at the feet of the king and pleaded for mercy. "I didn't steal this, O King! I found it on the ground where the boulder was. It must be yours. Please don't kill me!"

The king said, "Arise, My Son."

Shocked, the peasant slowly came to his feet. Afraid to make eye contact, he simply stared at the floor.

The king picked up the velvet bag and brought it to the peasant. He said, "Thank you, My Son, for moving the boulder. This bag of jewels and gold and silver is yours, and you are my heir. You shall be the next king on my passing because you had the courage to move the boulder!"

I don't know what fears and challenges you are facing as you read this. But this I do know: If you are willing to have the courage to move your boulder, there will be a treasure waiting for you at the end.

It may be riches and jewels, but it may simply be a great sense of satisfaction or accomplishment. It may be a good night's sleep, or the joy of a restored relationship, or loving the new job you have after leaving one that caused you endless stress and heartache.

It won't be easy. There will be setbacks. You will want to quit.

Several years ago, my wife and I watched the action/comedy movie *Knight and Day*[2] starring Tom Cruise and Cameron Diaz. Early in the movie when they first met, they were sitting across the aisle from each other on an airplane. They started a conversation that led to talking about things they hoped to do someday.

2 Knight and Day. Los Angeles, CA: 20th Century Fox, 2010. Film.

The Diaz character tells the story of a 1966 GTO she was restoring. She said, "I used to dream that someday when the last part went in, I would climb into that GTO, start it up, and just drive and drive and drive until I got to the tip of South America." Cruise brings the "someday" conversation to an abrupt end when he says, "Someday. That's a dangerous word. It's really just code for never."

Everyone reading this book has a someday. What is yours? What is it that you want to do *someday*? Will Cruise's words be prophetic in your life? Is your "someday" really code for "never"?

Courageous people go after their somedays! My challenge and encouragement to you as you finish this book is make *today* your *someday* for *something*.

Have the courage to share your story.
It will make a difference for someone else.

DAVE CORNELL

Chapter 12

Journeys of Courage

In what I hope will inspire you to take that first step toward removing your boulder, I will share a few stories about others who have gone before you. These are their stories.

Mary

The name on the email that day was unfamiliar to me. I opened it and was surprised by what I read. Her name was Mary and she had heard me speak a full year prior to my receiving the email from her. Her story is truly one of courageous action.

In her message to me, Mary stated that hearing me speak gave her very clear direction that she needed to act. For over eleven months, she had witnessed something that had bothered her but that she didn't do anything about it.

Mary was the director of a non-profit organization. Overseeing her role as the director was a board of directors. After hearing my presentation to an organization of her peers and colleagues, Mary said she knew she had to act and she knew the consequences for her actions would, potentially, lead to a difficult outcome for her.

This is how Mary described what she faced, in her own words:

At the time, I was dealing with a long-standing (and increasingly volatile) sexual-harassment issue between the president of my board and one of my staff. Your message encouraged me to do the right thing: Blow the whistle on the activities to protect my staff member. It didn't end well for me. The board rallied around the president and fired me for making a big deal out of it and "my not trusting" the board for decisions individuals made, allowing the situation to perpetuate.

There were a couple of significant factors at play in this scenario. First of all, this was taking place in a small community where "everyone knows everyone." Second, the president was quite a prominent and highly regarded person in this small town. These factors weighed heavily on Mary as she made her decision to act. She was well aware that bringing this harassment to light would likely lead to her termination and carry additional repercussions that she was unable to predict.

However, in spite of the potential damage to her position, career, and reputation, Mary knew she had to do the right thing. Four days after she had received her annual bonus, Mary was terminated from her position as the director of the organization.

I remember my reaction of horror as I read that she had lost her job. Initially I thought, "The intent in sharing my message is surely not to lead my audience to the ranks of the unemployed!" I hurt for Mary and wanted to take it all back.

As I processed through her email, though, I realized this is exactly what I want my message to be about. Courage is all about people taking steps they may not take otherwise. The consequences of those actions may be painful at times but, ultimately, they are actions that will make a positive difference in someone's life.

Mary did that. She stood up for her employee and it cost her, but it was the right thing to do. Mary went on to say in her first email to me:

Even though it didn't bode well for me (I kinda knew it wouldn't), I would feel much worse for not taking the high road, not doing the human thing, and agreeing to be a "whipped dog" by sweeping it all under the rug. And I know something better is on the way.

As I write this, it has been about two-and-a-half years since Mary took action. Shortly after her termination, Mary filed a wrongful termination lawsuit against the organization.

She has yet to find work that is in her field. In spite of all the challenges she has faced, Mary knows she did the right thing, the courageous thing.

In the course of her experience, Mary shared with me seven things she learned in her journey of courage. Here they are:

1. The short-term comfort of being cowardly will most likely

be eclipsed by extreme discomfort (by anxiety, by the ripple effect of other problems, by what happens if you're found out).

2. Forgiveness is a road. The most important thing is to get on it right away and fight to stay on it. (Heaven knows I've fallen off the shoulder many times!) You can't get anywhere positive unless you're actively on the road of forgiving yourself as well as others.

3. God needs time. Sometimes a lot. But, in the end, when He is ready, you will be amazed. Jaw-dropping, who-would-ever-think-that-would-happen amazed.

4. No one is above the need for compassion. There is nothing like being knocked down a few notches to see all the people who could use your compassion. It's free; give it generously. Courageously accept that you need it, too.

5. Let go of the things you can't control. Put them on God's to-do list and let it go. God is a great multi-tasker, so let Him manage it. There is a trust—and I would say courage—in believing God will work all things for good. Let Him.

6. Don't be a jerk. Spend your life making deposits in the Nice Guy Bank, not the United Bank of Jerks, and when you need to act bravely, everyone you know will be familiar with where you bank and what motivates your actions

7. The Land of Courage is a lonely place. It's bordered by Fingerpointer-ville, ShutUpAndDon'tLook-son, Don'tBelieveYou-town, and LetItGo. The very best friends will boldly visit you there and hold your hand.

This particular journey of courage is over for Mary. I'll let you hear the results, again, in her own words as she provided them to me:

After spending well over a year in the legal process, the road ended without a jury getting to decide the outcome. I had taken on the legal process so I could find out what really happened to me. Even though it was a tangled, complex knot, I found out at the very end what had transpired in the background of the whole situation. One of the most amazing things I learned on that long road was that a few days before I blew the whistle, a performance review for me had been drafted. It was glowing; the kind of review any employee would be proud to have.

While the whole legal process was unfurling, and unable to find a new non-profit leadership position, I went back to running a design business my husband and I started in 2004. Designing new homes, remodelings, and additions, I am spending my energy making people happy by creating places for them to raise a family, entertain, and live their lives. Regularly I get to witness people's daily lives made easier and more enjoyable because of my work with them. It is so rewarding to be a part of that. In addition, I get to work from home and be available to my kids after school or during the summer since I can make my own schedule, which is really valuable to me.

Looking back on the whole thing (a year now since it has all ended), I don't know that I am more consciously courageous, but I do know that:

- I am better at trusting God and His plan for me. I am more compassionate.

- Our culture has a very deep, serious issue with discrimination (read the local and national news if you think I am biased).

- I have some amazing, supportive friends and family.

- I am stronger than I thought. (I went for hours, toe-to-toe with the defense lawyers trying to trip me up, cut me down, and get me to thin down my story. It didn't work.)

- God is always, always with me. And you.

- Courage requires tears. And cussing. And naps.

I'd like to think I would be more courageous the next time I was faced with something as difficult as blowing the whistle and suffering the fallout. That doesn't mean I am going looking for a fight or a cause to pursue; I just think that now that I've seen the beginning/middle/end, the next time wouldn't be so scary if I were faced with as difficult of a situation.

But courage is about standing alone—even when the last person jumps ship and you know you're going down with the rig. It's about knowing you're going to be walking that ocean floor alone and that there are a lot of people who hope you never bubble back to the surface. But to continue the metaphor, I found a treasure chest under the water, and it's all mine and can't be stolen away. That's the prize in courage.

Bruce

Bruce called me up one day and asked me if I would join him for breakfast. We have a strong connection in that Bruce's son is married to my daughter. As a result, we share three grandchildren as well.

The call to meet him for breakfast was a bit unusual, but I didn't think it was out of the ordinary in any way. We had gotten together for meals before but it usually included other family members.

As we began, we shared some stories about the grandkids and the different funny, yet-adorable, things they had done. Then Bruce said he had something he wanted to share with me.

"I turned in my resignation at work today and I'm retiring. I don't think I would be doing this now if I hadn't heard you speak. Just about every day since I heard you, when I drive to work, I wonder why I'm continuing to do this. I don't need to work and it's not much fun to work there, and hasn't been for a while. I've probably been thinking about this for ten years. Your message made me realize it was time. Thank you."

It is a humbling thing to have people share these stories with me. I feel incredibly blessed to share a message that makes a difference in the lives of others. I am simply the messenger. Those taking action are the courageous ones.

Michele

Michele's story is not a result of her hearing me speak but rather a result of me hearing her speak! She is someone

I have admired and looked up to in building my business as a speaker. She is an amazing storyteller and one who has crafted a speaking business that regularly impacts and changes peoples' lives, including mine. You can find out more about her at www.michelecushatt.com

Michele has had her share of challenges in life. The tagline on her website is, "Making peace with an imperfect life." I first heard her speak at a conference I attended in November of 2014. She very candidly and openly shared about being divorced and remarried. She shared her struggles with multiple bouts of cancer. She is one of the most genuine, authentic, and sincere speakers I have ever heard.

I had the pleasure of hearing Michele at another conference I attended in October of 2015. At first, I was surprised she was there since I was aware that she had learned recently that her cancer was back.

Michele acted as the host and emcee for much of the conference. When she first stood up and started speaking, I quickly noticed that she had a speech impediment. I tried to mentally flash back to November of 2014 and remember whether she'd had it back then. Instead, I remembered that I had heard her multiple times on Michael Hyatt's podcasts and realized there was definitely something different about her speech.

One particular evening during the conference, Michele shared her story. It was a story that had changed dramatically since I had heard her in 2014. She began by telling us that her cancer came back for the third time in November of 2014, the month that I had first seen her. The prognosis wasn't good. Her description of what her body went through as she attempted to fend off the cancer again was heart-wrenchingly descriptive. You could hear the pain in her voice as she told us of how her body was wracked over and over again through the treatments.

Ultimately, this time they had to remove part of her tongue, where the cancer was located. Think of it! Michele had made her mark on the world as a speaker and an author. She spoke often at Christian women's conferences and was highly sought after and greatly esteemed in her field. And now her speaking voice had been severely impacted. As she spoke that night, she explained how she thought it was all over now. After all, who would want a speaker who can't speak very well? What would she do now?

After her treatments and surgery were completed and her cancer declared gone once again, she had the opportunity to go out for coffee with a couple of her girlfriends. She shared about what joy it brought her just to be out and enjoying being with friends and beginning to move forward.

While they were walking along and chatting, the women ran into another friend of theirs who was with her young daughter. The daughter listened quietly while the ladies talked. After hearing Michele, the little girl looked up at her and innocently asked, "Why do you talk so funny?" The question hit her hard and only deepened her thoughts that she would need to find another way to make her mark and share her message.

Michele is blessed to have a strong community of family and peer supporters who prayed for her and encouraged her to continue speaking in spite of her misgivings that anyone would want to hear someone who sounded as she did. She shared with us that night how this was her first presentation since deciding to speak again.

I vividly remember her telling us how scared she was when she got in her car to drive to the location of the conference in her home state. She got emotional as she described sitting in her car and not wanting to go, and of the great fear she felt pouring over her. She shared the similar comments that we all say to ourselves when we are afraid. "Why am I doing this? No one will want to hear me the way I sound now! I'm going to embarrass myself. Just turn the car around and go home."

Thankfully, for all of us in attendance, she didn't. Courageously, she put her foot on the gas pedal and drove to the conference center in spite of the fear that welled inside her.

I share Michele's story here because it so strongly supports two of my main points in this book. First, never underestimate the value of a crisis. No one would dare say that Michele's struggles with cancer were not a crisis in her life. We wouldn't want to go through what she did, nor would we wish those circumstances on anyone. Yet that crisis, I believe, has made Michele's story even more powerful. I held Michele in highest esteem prior to that conference in the fall of 2015, but now that esteem is even higher.

Michele's story prior to her third bout of cancer was amazing. Now her story of courage and perseverance is even stronger. Her ability to share her message in spite of what some might consider a flaw has been enhanced by that flaw. She has shown us that a crisis in our lives builds and strengthens our stories.

The second point Michele's story conveys is that it prompts us to ask ourselves, "Who pays the price for your fear?" As I listened to Michele tell her story of sitting in her car and the fear she felt about coming to the conference, I was overwhelmed. No one would have blamed her or called her a chicken if she had decided to turn around, head home, take her bags out of the car, and not go. She had a pretty good excuse if she wanted to use it.

But she didn't. She faced her fear and courageously made her way to the conference. I remember sitting in complete awe as I listened to her speak. What amazing courage it took to share her story. If Michele had not been there, the conference wouldn't have been as good. We likely wouldn't have known what we missed, but because she was there, we now had an awareness of what wouldn't have been if she hadn't faced her fear.

For Michele to withhold her story from us would have been selfish on her part. Her cancer and her speech impediment are part of her story and make her who she is. There is power in her story, and eliminating or hiding any of it would be an injustice to those who have the blessing of hearing her speak.

The parts of our stories that are most difficult for us to tell are the parts that make us so real and genuine and authentic to those we encounter in our everyday lives.

Joel

Joel is a young friend of mine from church. He is about the age of my own daughters.

He and his wife had recently moved from his hometown in Georgia to our small town in Minnesota to be closer to her family.

Joel began by telling me at our lunch meeting that he was very frustrated in his job. He just wasn't feeling challenged at all and often found himself looking for things to do because he got his work done so quickly.

I asked Joel if he'd talked about how he felt with his boss. He said he was afraid he would come across as a disgruntled employee. He felt he simply hadn't been there long enough to prove to his boss that he was worthy of something more.

I then asked him if he knew he was meeting the expectations they had of him. He said he was frequently being told he had done a good job and that they appreciated having him. Next I asked Joel how he thought his boss would know he was wanting something more, to which he replied, "I thought she would just know."

Then he reverted to his fears. "I'm afraid they'll think I'm too pushy or aggressive. I'm afraid I'll come across ungrateful for what I have. I'm afraid I'll get put into something I'm not ready for." We talked for a while longer and at the end of our lunch, Joel told me he would talk with his boss.

Later he shared with me that his boss was grateful he had approached her, that she did have some ideas for Joel, and that there were going to be some changes coming soon. Not long afterward, Joel told me he had received a promotion and attributed much of that promotion to his being courageously proactive in talking with his boss.

Mallory

Mallory began by telling me that, way back in 1991, she had said to herself, "Someday I would like to make salad for a living." Now, she found herself out of work with no job prospects. She happened to be attending a workshop where I was speaking to unemployed people about being courageous in the job search.

Maybe it was time to start to fulfill her "someday." By applying many of the things she heard me speak about and that I've shared in this book, Mallory had two job offers in the food-service industry within a very short period of time. Here is Mallory's description of what she did:

- I followed many of your ideas and, of course, they worked.

- I did scary stuff. (I contacted people I didn't know.)

- I addressed negative thoughts that prevented me from moving forward. (I have no culinary experience so why would they want *me*?)

- I posted quotes to help me stay positive. My current favorite is: "For every minute you are angry, you lose sixty seconds of happiness."—Ralph Waldo Emerson.

Because Mallory acted courageously by reaching out to people she didn't know, she received a call to attend an invitation-only job fair in the food-service industry. It is there that she had the opportunity to show her passion. She received both a full-time and a part-time job offer from two different companies.

Katie

Katie was serving as a communications intern at a non-profit organization during her final semester of college when she heard me speak. I'll let her words tell her story.

> I am currently serving as a communications intern and also finishing up my senior year of college. Needless to say, I am about ready to face a tremendous amount of change in my life: Graduation and a pretty intense job search.
>
> After hearing you yesterday, I realized I do have a fear—a *huge* fear that actually terrifies me beyond belief: The unknown. It is scary to think that I have no idea where I might be six months from now because I have always known what was ahead.
>
> It used to be that I would know that in the next year I would be in the next grade, and the year after that I would move up another grade level. Now I'm not sure where I'm going to end up. As a communications person, there are a whole lot of places I could go, yet there seems to always be that looming possibility of failure.
>
> I think your presentation was the exact message I needed to hear during this time of uncertainty in my life. I need a

new way to see how I could make my fear of the unknown into a positive outlook on change. Last night, I was having a conversation about my future with a close friend and I found myself telling your story about how you got glasses and chose not to wear them, sacrificing visual clarity because you were maybe afraid of the inconvenience they posed or the judgment you would receive.

As I recounted this story, I actually found myself being moved to tears as I had a bit of a revelation in that moment. I realized that, in order for me to have clarity with regard to my own future, I need to simply embrace the changes in my life just as you later did with your glasses. Sometimes change can be what is best for us; we don't need to be afraid of it—even if it is unknown.

I'm still not sure where I will end up or which direction I will take, but I am sure that putting a frame of positivity around the unknown will keep me from being scared.

In my response to Katie, I did remind her that she is likely to still be scared of the unknown but that she can embrace it and step into her fear. Remember, this book isn't about becoming fearless. I don't think that happens too often, if ever. This book is about becoming courageous and "saddling up" in spite of your fear.

It is not the critic who counts;
not the man who points out how the strong man stumbles, or where the doer of deeds could have done them better. The credit belongs to the man who is actually in the arena, whose face is marred by dust and sweat and blood; who strives valiantly; who errs, who comes short again and again, because there is no effort without error and shortcoming; but who does actually strive to do the deeds; who knows great enthusiasms, the great devotions; who spends himself in a worthy cause; who at the best knows in the end the triumph of high achievement, and who at the worst, if he fails, at least fails while daring greatly, so that his place shall never be with those cold and timid souls who neither know victory nor defeat."

THEODORE ROOSEVELT

Chapter 13

Conclusion

The great entrepreneur and motivational speaker, Jim Rohn, once said, "We must all suffer from one of two pains: The pain of discipline or the pain of regret. The difference is discipline weighs ounces while regret weighs tons."

I believe this quote fits so well in one's journey—to live courageously or to live in fear.

The pain of discipline reflects the courageous life. It's choosing to be uncomfortable to create a better result for yourself or for those around you, or both.

The pain of regret reflects choosing to live in fear and not stepping out courageously. The result is the constant nagging of the voice in your head telling you that you aren't worthy or don't deserve any better than what you have.

Ultimately, it all comes down to a choice. When you think about it, everything in life is a choice. We choose what we wear in the morning, we choose our attitudes, we choose how to treat people.

Some things happen in our lives that we don't choose, but how we react or respond to those situations involves a choice. Maybe it's an accident with long-term consequences or an illness that could prove to be debilitating or even deadly. We have a choice in how we live with those consequences or circumstances.

We can choose to be bitter. We can choose to complain and wonder, "Why me?" Or we can choose to look for a silver lining in the bleakest and darkest of clouds.

Fear and courage are choices as well.

People who choose to live in fear die in regret. They look back on their lives and think about all of the things they wish they had done or, at least, tried. They often live bitter or depressed lives as they compare themselves to others who choose to live in courage. They view others as being "lucky" or to have gotten all of the breaks. They see themselves as having had very little control over the direction their lives took.

People who choose to live courageously die knowing they at least tried. Maybe the results weren't what they had hoped, but they at least gave it a shot. Maybe their lives took a dramatic, positive change because they acted courageously and accomplished things they never saw as possible.

So, which person are you? Will you choose to live in fear—or choose to live courageously? The choice is yours!

Acknowledgments

There are so many people who have played a role in helping me get this project to completion. I'm sure I will neglect to mention some of them here, but their role is not minimized by my memory!

Early in this journey I had a counselor who helped me uncover a lot of things that were critical in helping me to recognize my need for courage. She shall remain nameless, but without her help, none of this would have happened.

Thank you to Catherine Byers Breet who first gave me the opportunity to give my presentation on fear and courage. You took a chance not having any idea what you would get for that risk. Your encouragement has been invaluable.

David Horsager, thank you for being a friend and more of a mentor than you realize. Getting to know you and work with you has helped me to grow in so many ways. I still marvel at the opportunity to know, and work with, you!

My editor and designer, Sue Filbin, has been amazing to work with on my first book. Sue, your patience and direction mean more than you know. I had no idea what I was doing and you took me on as a client anyway! Your encouragement through the process has been priceless!

Before Sue took on the project, I was introduced to another editor. Thank you, Sherry Miller, for taking a first run-through on this book. Your encouragement in letting me know you thought there was value in the book was critical.

Even before I began to speak on fear and courage, I had the great pleasure to meet Paul Bernabei and his Top 20 Training team. They introduced me to the concept of The FRAME, which is a critical part of my story and this book. Thank you for your permission to share this important lesson!

Dr. Ron Ross is a guy I have never had the opportunity to meet face-to-face. However, we have spent countless hours together online via Skype and Zoom. Ron, thank you for all of your encouragement as well as the times you have challenged me. You have been an inspiration to me in so many ways!

Thank you to the many people who have shared their stories of fear and courage with me. Some of those stories made it in the book and others didn't. It is humbling to have people say they are going to share something they have never shared with anyone else.

Thank you to Jan Haeg, John Warder, and Jim Lieske. Each of you, in your own way, are a part of this book and I am grateful for your presence in my life.

Thank you to my family: My wife, Amy, my children, Kaitlyn and Sara, my son-in-law Tyler, and my four grand-children—Hallie, Josiah, Troy, and Theo. May the rest of my life reflect more courage for you than the earlier years!

About the Author

Dave Cornell is the founder and president of Cultivate Courage, LLC, an organization dedicated to helping others overcome their fears and lead their most courageous life. Dave is a speaker, coach, and trainer focusing on personal development and leadership. He lives in Fergus Falls, Minnesota, with his wife Amy. They have two daughters, one son-in-law, and four grandchildren.